EDGE BOOKS

X-SPORTS

SKATEBOARDING

BY ERIC PRESZLER

Capstone
press

Mankato, Minnesota

Edge Books are published by Capstone Press
151 Good Counsel Drive, P.O. Box 669, Mankato, Minnesota 56002
www.capstonepress.com

Library of Congress Cataloging-in-Publication Data
Preszler, Eric.
    Skateboarding / by Eric Preszler.
       p. cm.—(Edge books. X-sports)
    Includes bibliographical references (p. 31) and index.
    Contents: Skateboarding—Skateboarding gear—Skateboarding moves—
Skateboarding stars.
    ISBN 0-7368-2712-9 (hardcover)
    1. Skateboarding—Juvenile literature. [1. Skateboarding.] I. Title. II. Series.
GV859.8.P74 2005
796.22—dc22   2003026973

Editorial Credits
Tom Adamson, editor; Jason Knudson, designer; Jo Miller, photo researcher;
    Eric Kudalis, product planning editor

Photo Credits
Capstone Press/Gary Sundermeyer, 12 (both)
Corbis/Bettmann, 6; NewSport/Steve Boyle, 8, 27; NewSport/Al Fuchs, 17;
    NewSport/Rick Rickman, 25; NewSport/X Games IX/Matt A. Brown, 28;
    Reuters NewMedia Inc., 11
Getty Images/Nick Laham, 5; Tom Hauck, 9; Elsa, 19 (top), 20
SportsChrome Inc., cover; Mike Ehrmann, 14, 19 (bottom), 21

**Edge Books thanks Tod Swank, member, Board of Directors, International
Association of Skateboard Companies, for his assistance in preparing this book.**

1 2 3 4 5 6 09 08 07 06 05 04

TABLE OF CONTENTS

CHAPTER 1

SKATEBOARDING

The skateboarder balances on top of the halfpipe. He gazes down at the smooth wooden surface. Slowly, he rolls to the edge. His wheels squeak to a sudden stop. The crowd becomes silent.

He drops into the halfpipe. In no time, he is soaring down the U-shaped curve. The halfpipe walls launch him straight into the air. The first trick of his run is a handplant. The skater grabs the coping with his right hand. He grabs his board with his left hand. He glides back down the ramp and gets ready for his next move.

LEARN ABOUT:

- A halfpipe trick
- Early skateboards
- Skateboarding's founders

The handplant is an impressive skateboarding move.

Skateboarding became popular in the early 1960s.

EARLY SKATEBOARDING

The idea of skateboarding dates back to the early 1900s. People attached roller-skate wheels to wooden planks. They connected scooterlike handles to the front of the boards.

By the late 1950s, skateboarders had removed the scooter handle. In 1959, the first skateboards hit the stores. Over the next five years, the sport's popularity exploded.

The new sport attracted many surfers. At that time, skateboarding was called sidewalk surfing. Larry Stevenson supported skateboarding in his magazine *Surf Guide*.

UPS AND DOWNS

By the mid-1960s, skateboarding's popularity declined rapidly. Too many low-quality skateboards were made. The cheap clay wheels didn't provide good control. People lost interest in the sport.

Stevenson and Frank Nasworthy improved skateboards and helped save the sport. Stevenson invented the kicktail in the late 1960s. This curved part on the rear of the skateboard helped skaters control the board better.

Bob Burnquist helped make skateboarding popular at the X Games.

Nasworthy put smooth urethane wheels on skateboards. The new wheels lasted longer. By 1973, skateboarding was popular again.

More improvements soon followed. Wider boards gave riders more control. In the 1970s, people began to build skateboard parks. Competitions also became popular.

In the early 1980s, skateboarding hit a standstill again. Some cities banned skateboarding. BMX racing and other action sports became more popular. Skaters lost interest in flatland freestyle and downhill skating.

In the late 1980s, streetstyle and vert skating became popular. By 1995, skateboarding was on TV thanks to the X Games.

Skateboarding is still changing and growing. Skaters keep the sport interesting and enjoyable.

Andy Macdonald is a star vert skater.

CHAPTER 2

SKATEBOARDING GEAR

A skater needs more than just a skateboard. Beginners should wear knee, elbow, and wrist pads. All skaters should wear a helmet and durable shoes.

SKATEBOARDS

A skater stands on a wooden board called a deck. The deck is about 30 inches (76 centimeters) long. Most decks are made of seven thin layers of maple wood. Layers make the board strong. Many skaters add stickers or designs to their decks.

LEARN ABOUT:

- Decks
- Wheels
- Safety gear

Skaters add their own style to their skateboards' designs.

Skateboard wheels are now made of urethane.

Metal trucks hold the wheels.

Decks have a slight rise at both ends. The front of the deck is called the nose. The back of the deck is the tail. The nose and tail are used to perform tricks.

On the bottom of the deck, two metal pieces called trucks hold the wheels. The size and material of the wheels vary. Skaters who want to skate fast usually use large, hard wheels. Street skaters use smaller hard wheels for better control. Soft wheels add control and grip. These wheels are used for park skating.

EDGE FACT

Some skaters ride longboards. Longboards are best for cruising down hills. These boards are 60 inches (152 centimeters) long.

Helmets and pads help prevent injuries.

PADS AND SHOES

Skateboarding involves high speeds and risky tricks. Skaters crash often. Knee and elbow pads help make injuries less serious. Most pads are made of foam covered with plastic.

The helmet is a skater's most important piece of protective equipment. One out of every five skateboarding injuries is to the head. Helmets protect skateboarders from serious head injuries.

Skateboarders should wear durable shoes that provide good traction. Traction helps skaters control the board and perform tricks.

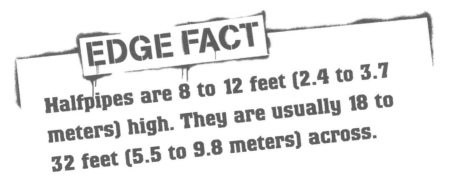

EDGE FACT

Halfpipes are 8 to 12 feet (2.4 to 3.7 meters) high. They are usually 18 to 32 feet (5.5 to 9.8 meters) across.

CHAPTER 3

SKATEBOARDING MOVES

The number of skateboarding tricks is limited only by skaters' imaginations. Skaters do tricks on railings, ramps, sidewalks, halfpipes, and bowls. The sport never gets boring.

BASIC TRICKS

The ollie is an important basic trick. Almost all aerial tricks start with an ollie. A skater first places the back foot on the board's tail. The front foot stays on the center of the board. The skater stomps down on the tail to make the nose pop up.

LEARN ABOUT:
- The ollie
- Grinds and slides
- Tailgrab

Skaters ollie up to an obstacle to perform tricks.

The skater then slides the front foot up to the nose of the board while lifting the rear foot. The board looks like it is attached to the skater's feet.

Grinds and slides are popular moves. To grind or slide, a skater must first ollie up to an obstacle. A grind is when a skater drags one or both metal trucks across an obstacle. A nosegrind uses the front truck and the board's nose. A 50-50 grind is a grind across both trucks.

A slide is when a skater drags the deck across a railing or other obstacle. A boardslide drags the middle of the board across an obstacle. A skater uses the nose of the board to do a noseslide. When a skater uses the board's tail, it's a tailslide.

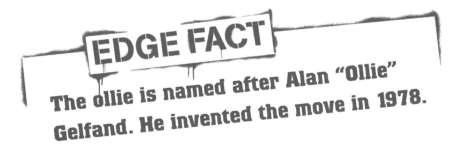

EDGE FACT

The ollie is named after Alan "Ollie" Gelfand. He invented the move in 1978.

A frontside 50-50 grind uses both trucks to grind on an obstacle.

A frontside boardslide uses the middle of the board to slide.

19

ADVANCED TRICKS

Many skateboarding tricks are challenging. Grabs and aerials are popular but difficult tricks. Pro skaters even do rotations up to 900 degrees, or two and one-half spins.

The best skaters do aerials. They often do grabs during aerials. While in the air, they may hold the tail of the board. This move is called a tailgrab. Holding the nose of the board is a nosegrab. Some skaters can do an Indy air. While in the air, they grab the toe edge of the board with the back hand.

A skater grabs the board's tail for a tailgrab.

For a varial, the skater rotates the board under the feet.

Other aerials involve spinning or flipping the board. For a varial, skaters spin the board. The board faces the opposite direction after landing. For a kickflip, skaters flip the board with their feet.

The best skaters combine tricks. The Indy air becomes a kickflip Indy when skaters add a kickflip to the move. Skaters also can do a spin while doing a tailgrab or nosegrab.

HOW TO DO A
FRONTSIDE 180

3. For the half spin, the skater must twist the body around.

4. The skater lands facing the opposite direction, using the arms to maintain balance.

CHAPTER 4

SKATEBOARDING STARS

Many skateboarders have become famous after competing in the X Games or Gravity Games. New stars also keep the sport popular. No one has helped make skateboarding popular more than Tony Hawk.

TONY HAWK

Tony Hawk received his first skateboard when he was 9 years old. He rolled into a fence on his first try. He practiced often and learned quickly. At age 11, he entered his first contest.

Hawk turned pro a few years later. He struggled at first. With every loss, he practiced more. By age 15, he was the National

LEARN ABOUT:
- Tony Hawk
- Andy Macdonald
- Ryan Sheckler

Tony Hawk is an expert at spectacular vert tricks.

Skateboard Association (NSA) World Champion. He continued to dominate the NSA titles until the early 1990s.

Hawk has created at least 80 tricks. He has won 16 medals in the X Games. He also owns Birdhouse Skateboards, which makes skateboards and other equipment.

ANDY MACDONALD

Andy Macdonald turned pro in 1995. Starting in 1996, Macdonald won the World Cup overall combined title five years in a row. The combined title includes both streetstyle and vert skating. Macdonald is also a 14-time medalist in the X Games and stars in a skateboarding video game.

In 1999, Macdonald set a world distance record on a skateboard. He soared 52 feet, 10 inches (16.1 meters). He completed this jump without crashing.

EDGE FACT

Danny Way holds the new distance record. In 2002, he landed a 65-foot (20-meter) jump.

Andy Macdonald performs a frontside tailslide during a vert event.

Ryan Sheckler won the park event at the 2003 X Games.

Macdonald is both an excellent skater and a good role model. In 1999, he joined President Bill Clinton for a speech supporting the Partnership for a Drug-Free America.

YOUNG STARS

Lyn-Z Adams Hawkins began pro skating at age 12. She took second in the bowl competition at the 2002 Mervyn's Beach Bash in Hermosa Beach, California. In a 2002 X Games demo, Hawkins was the youngest of four female skaters.

Ryan Sheckler is the youngest skater to win a major event. In 2003, he won the gold medal in the park event at the X Games. He was 13 years old. Sheckler started competing at age 7. He often appears with Tony Hawk at demos and events. Some people say Sheckler could be as successful as Hawk someday.

GLOSSARY

coping (KOH-ping)—the top edge of a halfpipe ramp

deck (DEK)—the wooden part of a skateboard that a skater stands on

halfpipe (HAF-pipe)—a U-shaped ramp with high walls used for vert skating tricks

park (PARK)—a style of skateboarding involving tricks on bowls, ramps, walls, and other obstacles

streetstyle (STREET-stile)—a style of skateboarding involving tricks on sidewalk and street obstacles; these obstacles can include railings, benches, picnic tables, and steps.

truck (TRUHK)—the part of a skateboard that attaches the wheels to the deck

urethane (YUR-uh-thayn)—a hard plastic used to make skateboard wheels

vert (VURT)—a style of skateboarding involving tricks done in a halfpipe

READ MORE

Herran, Joe, and Ron Thomas. *Skateboarding*. Action Sports. Philadelphia: Chelsea House, 2003.

Powell, Ben. *Skateboarding*. Extreme Sports. Minneapolis: Lerner, 2004.

Savage, Jeff. *Tony Hawk: Skateboarding Legend*. Skateboarding. Mankato, Minn.: Edge Books, 2005.

INTERNET SITES

FactHound offers a safe, fun way to find Internet sites related to this book. All of the sites on FactHound have been researched by our staff.

Here's how:

1. Visit *www.facthound.com*
2. Type in this special code **0736827129** for age-appropriate sites. Or enter a search word related to this book for a more general search.
3. Click on the **Fetch It** button.

FactHound will fetch the best sites for you!

INDEX